ALL THE TIMES WE PASSED
MCDONALD'S BETWEEN CHAPEL HILL
AND TUXEDO, NORTH CAROLINA

❈

ALL THE TIMES WE PASSED
MCDONALD'S BETWEEN CHAPEL HILL
AND TUXEDO, NORTH CAROLINA

✻

ANDREW DALLY

NEW MICHIGAN PRESS
TUCSON, ARIZONA

NEW MICHIGAN PRESS
DEPT OF ENGLISH, P. O. BOX 210067
UNIVERSITY OF ARIZONA
TUCSON, AZ 85721-0067

<http://newmichiganpress.com>

Orders and queries to <nmp@thediagram.com>.

Copyright © 2019 by Andrew Dally.
All rights reserved.

ISBN 978-1-934832-66-0. FIRST PRINTING.

Printed in the United States of America.

Design by Ander Monson.

Cover image courtesy of Jason Cimon:
http://www.jasoncimon.com.

CONTENTS

[I think it begins as a joke.] 1

5:21 2

5:30 3

5:32 4

-:-- 5

5:36 7

5:41 9

5:46 10

5:56 11

6:06 12

6:11 13

6:21 15

6:58 16

7:01 17

7:03 18

7:05 19

7:17 21

7:23 23

7:31 24

7:35 26

7:36 27

7:41 28

7:56 30

7:59 31

Notes 33

I think it begins as a joke. I am driving with Kian. We want McDonald's. We want to wrap our wanting in farce or want to want something we can have whenever we want it. *What* becomes *which*, becomes *out-of-how-many*, becomes a kind of wager, my timekeeping an averment. We had lived together for two years and not talked for two after, had taken in a dog adept at escape which we raised by turning loose. The dog could sprint for hours, for days. He seemed like everything seemed: inexhaustible. I think it begins as a joke. I am driving with Kian. Our dog is old and stays with my parents. In a red car beside us, a red car pulling ahead, our wives are not yet our wives. In a little red car, not far, Alison. I think it begins before, but it may begin after. In order to reverse-engineer a working simulation of love, it was necessary to break down all aspects of the original. The road stretches. Our potentials are downshifting tenses. My decisions begin to feel like memories. My memories begin to feel like dreams. I think. It begins as a joke. One day you find a list of timestamps in your phone and know this is how it all passed, like one McDonald's after another.

5:21

the southern city bleeds   out into the blank bolt   of farmfield it was once   the long parallels unstitch and go white i see lots   i see more lots   upturned and unpaved   pending or abandoned   the southern city bleeds out   and what can we do   but bleed out with it   thru the suburban subconscious   to the excerpted exurbs   a landscape of sleeper towns   for a populace of somnambulists   enclosed in my boxy apartment   all winter i grew   more susceptible to the vertical-   horizontal illusion   a certain smallness the wide open imposes   a fourth lane   foreshortens the horizon   i feel July   thick with on-deck rain   i feel the mildewy air   blow cold my bare ankles   did you see that McDonald's?   i feel like i lost   count before i could start counting   i feel like that must be enough   feelings for one poem

hey purplish catchfly
coughing up exhaust   at sway
in wide median

5:30

fifteen minutes in   Kian's 98 Protegé   doubles as fog machine
as storm supplants humidity   three months in   Bashō is
*putting up with heat and rain   spirit sore afflicted   taken ill
no way to keep writing*   in Japan   people call the Protegé
the Familia   in Iran   people pronounce Kian better
when i say Kian   i mean *the one   with soiled yesternapkins
scrubbing a fogged-over windshield   the one pointing his expensive
camera   at each M-shaped beacon   the one who keeps us mostly
on the road*   but more generally it means royalty   it means
six years earlier   i was expecting something   more marbled
more columnar   at the naturalization ceremony   when they
wheel   in a cowboy president   on a discount Japanese TV
and he belches *America   the Beautiful* the final test   is not to
laugh   if you crack   a window it means   the fog billows
out but the rain slants in   if you crack a window   and the
scent out there is the answer   to the dirt's parched prayers
is it more pleasant   for its ornately Greek name?   is the
name more perfect   if it's left unsaid?   *if it's not   too much
trouble   Kian could you keep your hands   on the goddamn
wheel?*   he says *if we crash*

*you tell them i died
how i lived   you tell them i
died multitasking*

5:32

a car-shaped gale   roils a car-shaped sea   a car-shaped sea courses our car-shaped car   our car cuts calculi in the woven elements   stirs up these small weathers   as a gradient layer cake   of speeds radiates away   i read equations on the internet   that i understand completely   on an emotional level   some moments feel more viscous   some drag is characterized as parasitic   the outside tries its best to keep up   as our rearview rewinds   the splotched drive home on the windshield and hood   crash drops of self-destructive rain   they dance   they disappear   into their dance partners   dark arcs   dark arcs   wipers so sinister   in their monotonous suppression   of the amoebic legions   of water reaching   for a freedom that lies   just outside the frame   when the rain sprays mistily   from car back to sky is it rain again?   a small envelope of air   cradles every tumbling droplet   the droplets expand   the landscape as they sew it   all together   you wake up   in a blacked-out America   and someone flashes on   a McDonald's sign   i am five   hundred thousand drops of rain   from home

i am only three
identical McDonald's
from where we first met

-:--

sun cook my laptop   laptop fry my thighs   recline with
me thighs   in this funny lawnchair wherein   we have no
choice   it's Mississippi   Alison cocooned in her sweaty
hammock   our new dog bounces cricket-like   after who
knows?   a cricket?

the spring releases
a minor version update
into the backyard

of twenty greens my browser
knows by name   out here I count

LawnGreen SpringGreen no
MediumSpringGreen   trees still
trembling with whitespace

trying to remember i click   thru stitched imageries   of
highway   for places to suture to times   trying to remember
the difference   between remembrance and revision   i drive
circles   in a machine's panoramic diary   i am   a damp
passenger seat   five years ago   i am behind   the wheel
of a driverless car   i am my body   when the breeze thru
the yard   up from the hollow shoulder   that was a red rain
puddle   in the ripped up clay   they've raised like a memory
a brand new McDonald's

Mississippi sun
sets over gulley so set
the car in reverse

5:36

somewhere outside Pittsburgh   sometime in the 60s   the Big Mac is born   somewhere outside Pittsburgh sometime in the 60s   so is my mother   twenty years later   outside New Iberia   they throw my father   into jail   over byways over bayous he is going over   a-hundred-an-hour   for a Big Mac for my mother   and for me for i am   swimming about her body somehow   my lungs all full of ketchup somewhere outside my mother   sometime in the 80s   i am born somewhere outside   a McDonald's   so is the PlayPlace   everyday my mother places me   in the PlayPlace so i can play   so she can eat her Big Mac   the little brown birds   sing *ketchup ketchup*   because they want to share my food i understand   they like french fries   because they are called french fry birds   i understand my PlayPlace   is different from McDonaldland   which is on TV   which is a place   with a clown and a thief   and a purple lumpy monster where a Big Mac goes by Officer Big Mac   i understand there   must be laws and orders there   i don't understand everything   in McDonaldland is a copy   but a judge waves his hammer and says   *both lands are governed*   *by officers with disproportionately*   *large round heads*   somebody steals   an imaginary somewhere   and looses it into the wavy air   now somewhere   on the internet   you can buy a decommissioned Officer   Big Mac jungle-gym   climb a ladder thru his body up into his head   and there you are   trapped inside a giant burger   a burger that is also a jail   a jail that is also a mouth

*dominant topo-
graphical features of these
locales are the same:*

*trees, caves, road, castle
a forest of talking trees
with human faces*

5:41

an american
flag gives the balmy highway
a bit too much tongue

big enough to sell a car
big enough to cause a wreck

the cellphone tower
dressed up like a giant cross
casts a cross shadow

and eavesdrops on the county's
clamor of short-wave prayers

a chemical light
like the firefly's silent
bodysong burning

burns thru the clouds   the yellow
sign arches its perverse back—

i want McDonald's
every moment like this
barely, completely

5:46

we pass exactly one McDonald's   for every four-point-one-seven minutes   of on-and-on-ness   in an ill-lit corrugated cubicle   in Oak Brook, Illinois   a level three analyst models our hunger   over distance   his spreadsheets spill over   his hard drive chirps   like ants munching dirt   his computer hums   and whirs like bees   patiently dying   the charts say more cheeseburgers   the powerpoints   say more powerpoints   the footnotes say coefficient   the footnotes say   remainder   the commute back to Aurora   back to his wife   their two daughters

    digital prints pinned—
    snowman sandcastle leafpile—
    into carpet wall

will take thirty-two minutes   each one passes   like a McNugget swallowed whole

5:56

It is 5:56. It is the last day of June. It is the last June of 2013. In a few moments a wildfire swallows nineteen firefighters in Arizona. In a few days the protests in Egypt end in coup. In North Carolina the rain is pummeling what it can find, while Kian and I speak of McDonald's. Yes, they are everywhere, but perhaps not as everywhere as we thought. I record every emergence with the urgency of the courtroom artist who dreams himself on trial. When I rediscover the timestamps in a discarded phone years later, they have taken on the appearance of a lost thing found. In this way they resemble all other lost things. In this way they seem like a poem or they seem like a dog. They seem like a poem about a dog.

Kian and I in the same car to the shelter. A slight and skittish hound. Maybe six years earlier. Maybe twenty pounds. We thought we'd play house. We thought we'd play master. We thought to play a game of ping-pong to see who got to name him. We knew I would lose. When you name a dog Argos, you name a dog that is going to die.

6:06

as the McDonald's spread themselves   thinner my panic wafts over the drowning landscape   as the timestamps recede into memory   a clustering and greenflash   as your particles drift apart in a hey   -don't-worry-about-it kind of way   as raindrop as field and static and crow fly   as in their wet casements run the powerlines birdless   as the machine wonders   don't you mean powerless bridles?   as a matter of fact i   as a point of reference i   as the words settle like blunt stones   in a skull or as we dust   the stone turning it in our palms   a stone-shaped mass   of disturbed earth   as the stone skips   across the water and the water   remembers the stone   a stone in a play of concentrics   as the water forgets   in one last yawning zero as Bashō writes

what was composed
on the fan wrenched apart
subsides together

does he write here   of his journey   or the three years it took to write it?   as i write a*s Bashō writes*   as in your head   i borrow your head's voice   and ask another harmless question

6:11

a new sign punctures
the rain-gauzed evening   haloed
in a Gaussian fog

nightlight-like they appear   lighthouse-like   how might
we fumble for the bathrooms   of our monstrous interiors
without   humping a knee *smack* there's the tub without
screaming awake our dreaming neighbors without   these signs
prying open this muddled space   would the space be space at
all?   or some sort of doorless hallway   filled with landscape
canvases   impossible to traverse without   shredding them
one by one by one *bye-bye*   as we step heedless thru?   i
don't know   the hypothetical exists without   me the stone
of grueling yearning   is lying   facedown in rice paddies
by the time Bashō arrives the villagers   rolled it ages ago
down the silent mountainside   so Bashō heaves   his
inch-space of heart   onward into the early modern hemlock
forests   their immensity perhaps   real but really   felt as
illusion   obstructed view   shifting sameness   the space
seems   to endlessly expand   as it shuts down around him
the without   draws itself from within   his little inch-space
the without   humming like the signs humming   their blunt
yellow anaphora   into the storm-soaked dusk   the signs
moistening their lips like   *mmmmmm mmmmmm* the signs
unfurling the earth like *me-me-me*   like *me-me-me-me-me*

the signs and the light
they pour us the light doing
all that stuff light does

6:21

i constructed a borderland   i made it from borders   so that it might have none   i covered my landscape in nightlights and love   the dreamscape it's become   our lives   thriving on a treadmill-like logic   i escape the conjured monster   to stand there   in a field of monstrous clover   fingering my monstrous particles   a McDonald's sign breaks   over the horizon   as another McDonald's sign   is released from the rearview   whenever Argos did escape   he'd appear to Kian   in panic-stoned visions   *lazing under the taqueria dumpster!*   *surrounded by bastards*   *he pisses all over frat court!*   whenever the dog returned he'd sleep for days   his exploits replaying on the rug   paw twitch and quiver lip   let me pet away each snarl   i'd massage his ear   i'd speak his world   i walked right into his dreams and right out and my dreams became porous like his   my dreams became those of a dog   i smelled my master all over them   when Argos dies he'll finally stay   dead in my dreams   but each night i dream alive   a perfect replica he is   the same in every way   but he is after   in my dreams he is asleep

i stroke his stomach
churning with dreams and feel it
for seams and stitches

6:58

the McRib Farewell
Tour marks the McRib's return
a seasonal treat

if cheap pork's your fav season
is this autumn? arbitrage?

the market removes
its hand from the meat grinder
to wind back the clocks

ribbed as in for your pleasure
or ribbed as in all ripped out?

reconstitute me
remove every bone and place
me in my bonesuit

7:01

initiate highway exit protocol   flash and whatever   is the inverse of merge   slice / disassociate   instantiate   one McDonald's zero-point-wherever   miles off offramp   raze and pave the particulars   raise up the skeletal beamwork of memory   brick by brick   lay down my deja vu   pump thru some sugar and meat   call up the contractor   call all the masons and Platonists   someone get a plumber   on the line   *hello?* can somebody please connect me   to Proust? the simulation spun-up at least an hour   at least sixty years prior a thousand locations-past materialize around us in convenient succession   all identical all impossible   to enter impossible to be here   and not there and there   but Kian here we are i guess   and of course they're here first   how shameful how sinister   it all seemed then   the smallest red car   resting in the lot   its aura of already there-ness   the niche domesticity a tuition covers   a time to adopt a dog   a time to buy a house a time to pull up to the window and deliver your order   your ironic Big Macs   your neurotic vacations   your Amazon boxes and HBO specials   kitchen gadgets   safety features

Alison thighs dressed
with fries sun fries thru round glass
salt me may this last

7:03

Kian garlands the dash   in dripping paper and cardboard the Cola bubbles as thru us it descends   cheers   here's to another hundred miles of tongue   massaging the fat-fuzzed palate   here's to the sugars coming undone   along their intricate zippers   something in me uncorks   a long insulin river   the brain doles out its chemical rewards   the pump and bellows fall out of phase   is my body like a McDonald's because inside it we discover   another outside?   or is my body like a McDonald's   because it survives on other bodies? o   -vercomplicated worm   o cavernous spelunker   o carnivorous donut   howdy Officer Big Mac   won't you come in?   my body is nothing   but doors and the water   is just right   you know i've never been   a french-fry kind of person

flesh smothered in flesh
colored sauces   we're swimming
a slurry of meat

7:05

Big Mac french fries and
Coke for only six bucks wow
that's Extra Value

But the mystic whispers *paradox* toward the drive-thru's crackling ear. How can a thing contain more value than it's assigned? *You value good food just as much as you value a good price* quips the adman. His crystal ball's all reflection, but hey partner, isn't that a kind of multiplication, too? In 2016, a Chicagoan sues the company upon realizing he can buy the parts (cheeseburger, cheeseburger, french fry, soft drink) for less than than the whole (a #4, thanks). *It's not about the 41 cents*, he tells the papers, *it's about what's right*. He might have said, it's about a different type of value. For example, across the board of your middle school math class someone draws a line, adorns it with integers—13, 5, 0, -7— because the *absolute value* of any number is best understood in terms of distance. Meanwhile, a music instructor down the hall strikes her piano. *Note value*, she explains, is all about duration. At first this all feels right: value—number to number or moment to moment—must be a way for us to talk about separation, but something nags at us. The remainder of the blackboard, clouded with the erasure of yesterday's equations. The infinite length of line left undrawn. That peculiar silence before the classroom launches into song. We step out on value's bridge and discover it's an island—something ungraspable at the transaction's perfect center. Some sign-light—red-yellow-white-light—glimmers in the rain and fog. Tree shapes scatter and wave thru the window-water. All these unbracketed data, all this extra value rinses the moment like a salve.

7:17

when we use time   as a measurement of distance   we assume a certain speed of motion   when the distances simply repeat   it's difficult to say we're still moving   when the whole drive sputters to a standstill   the digits on the radio-clock go aquiver   when we interrupt this broadcast   with a few words from our sponsors   we return speaking   in our sponsors' unplaceable tongues   when your mother reads   for the part of my mother   it makes sense doesn't it?   because no one cries   quite like the reader's mother?   when to weep my tears   they hire the handsome youth   test-markets are positive   he's too tall for the part   when my double just lies there   on the floor and the cameraman   gets confused we pan and we zoom   we come in close on his face

the boy on his knees
the dead animal and ear
he kneads for an hour

cue tracked giggles   strike a minor key   gently finger the holy diminished triad   O Argos i called upon the Lord   of Suburban Ordinances and Bylaws   and i just cannot   bury you beneath mommy   and daddy's parking pad   thus be enclosed in this irony machine   of nostalgia and deferment instead   let us bend your quickly stiffening body   into that gaudy M-shape   let us see you loping   in the windows and the mirrors   of every vehicle on every interstate   o sweet

goose!　　ma petite pomme de terre!　　o my amber McNugget
i know you hate car-trips　　so i buy you endlesss Happy Meals
the yuppies they hate this　　but i love you and you love　　to
eat garbage the yuppies　　they hate this but i love you　　and
neither of us ever has to go　　back to Seattle

7:23

duty thru duty abandoned   love thru owned love   sequence thru death and death   thru   replaceable life   grief thru repeatable death or life   thru a loose chronology   a hurried concatenate   as landscape thru window   so perfectly see-thru   so see "to work thru"   a cut-thru or thruway or the land   thru a map   to look or thumb   as in right thru the map   thru mirror and screen   thru sickness as in   it somehow just slipped thru the cracks   as in thru and thru leaf thru   leaves thru   left thru   thru which i mean to say   this language thru purchase   speaks thru me   or is this really me speaking   thru my ass?   my ass only ever passing thru   this life thru purchase   this duty thru a duty to purchase   thru the lungs a song of purchased grief   thru the wind and rain   thru moment and drive-

i bought a thing   it
died   so i learned and wept so
i bought another

7:31

overloaded clouds
looked not to advance at all
fear followed after

here i am rearranging
plucking song and syllable

some piled double
words vaguely made out through moss
a path amid fields

a dozen translations of
oku no hosomichi

the one poem left on
a pile of dead butterflies
each breath a last one

and there another hundred
invented demarcations

its momentariness
though contorted by nature
newly refurbished

stone and brand—disciples raised
franchises across the land

vermillion-lacquered
become the great edifice
paper standards   this occurred

when his master died Bashō
moved where he could get a job

centuries floated
from eye-cover to ear-flap
well, this must be it

7:35

in Asheville there's a McDonald's   that looks like a chalet   it's the only thing there is   to say about Asheville   twenty-five miles later there's Clyde   where cows and a paper mill churn in the mountains   people like their paper like people   like their ghosts   dead white   so the mill farts a bedsheet   of sulfites over the county   eyeholes snipped out for everyone to see people like me   like their cows wrapped in paper   thus cornfeed and grazeland   thus the heifer beams her methane farts into the climate models   and a jubilee of microflora goes apeshit   in the grandest chamber   of her baroque gut   o complexity   ain't so tough   all these small dumb things and each doing whatever it wants   how sad the wind-whipped blade of grass   looks hanging for life   while the whole hillock shimmers   waving stately in the breeze   when the heifer comes down with hardware disease   you don't overthink it   you run   grab the cow magnet   in one chamber there's a bible   in another there's a beehive   in one chamber a loose nail   inches closer to her heart

Kian knows a guy
from Clyde says in Clyde there's no
McDonald's at all

7:36

the oil rinses clean   from the asphalt like mud   from the heifers slick hides   and chickens stare straight   thru their swelling reflections   as shit-bogs flood over in the hog farms but dammed up in a server farm   our data lies dryly   the shadow   of a summer storm   spreads over three states   a shadow   of the self   washes over the networks   based on your interest   in *The Collected Poetry of Jack Spicer*   we've got great deals   on time machines   yah they run like a dream   but these old radios are a little finicky   past-purchase viewed-page used-credit   clicked-banner   five stars   Congratulations   because you rated *A History of Violence*   more history   more violence   please enjoy these several releases   related to   hog farm poultry farm server farm hog farm   Congratulations a past made   animate to sell its own future   a history extended   buffet-style before you   hog farm highway hog farm cloudburst shadowfarm history   come to life for you   to eat   because you purchased   a history   because your history   includes this purchase this purchase includes   this future because you purchased   Cid Corman's translation   of *Back Roads to Far Towns*

Congratulations
you won Congratulations
your shadow you won

7:41

over a million   more than five   billion burgers   billions and billions of burgers served worldwide   we couldn't keep up   with the old analog signs   more burgers sold   begot more burgers selling   on the claim they were sellable   as what was said became news   became whatever was tellable how could you   not try it? how could you   not like what's designed to be likable   won't you join me for a drink?   i'm having everything that's drinkable   my agency   having collapsed   into adjectives and adverbs   i moved like a double-agent   to a new life in the exurbs   the long drives were driverless and hard   work was workerless   but the meat was still meaty   it was derived from beefy animals   i wanted to explain things   that seemed inexplicable   so i spent all my money   on a small god of description   in order to know me   it needed a memory   so we gave it a language and we switched   on the power   and it began whirring then it began talking   it breathed *blip-blip blip*   over all my swirling waters   and it was good   seeming it was streaming in trueish   i was bleeping i was blooping   i was hued a red-green-blueish   when i drowned   in a plastic rainbow   i emerged huffing socksmell   my human mother raised me in a PlayPlace   at least i can play well   i eat cargo nets and vertical   i chow down on fecal-particulate   how can you tell me it's not edible   right after i ate it?   how can you   say it's not hatable   when i'm positive i hate it? how can you tell me   they're razing all the PlayPlaces?   those spaces aren't replaceable   i'm telling you   my human mother raised me there   it's tellable i'm telling you   my human mother raised me human   it's tellable   i'm telling you my human mother

7:56

ground and sky passing
water back and forth like no
one cares who keeps it

interstates slow to puddles
reflections hide painted lines

creeks run like rivers
rivers run like highway plans
rushing to become

rain keeps happening all week
the weeks just keep happening

7:59

A detour—a dirt road tracing the jagged northeast inlet—when we finally reach the lake. Kian pulls the car up to the weedy shoreline, as the storm, in jest or indifference, switches suddenly off. A text from Alison: How have we fallen so far behind? Something vague and reassuring I transmit back to the atmosphere. Syrupy ice-melt from soggy paper cups as our asses hum on the front bumper. Kian gazes out across the fog and steam like a boy who wants you to ask what holds his gaze. The valley of bugs loses its collective shit

between a sunset
raw burger spilt chemical
on water as sky

Out the open passenger door, an electric voice moans *air crickets air crickets air*, and I'm like, okay, is everyone in on this joke? It's the humidity, maybe, that's turned the world into a massive superconductor. For a moment, I love every dumb thing singing for its immunity to my song. For a moment, I love every dumb thing inside me for this grotesque simulation of love. For a moment—I crumble these napkins and receipts into a bag stained translucent with grease—I am sure I have been given exactly what I ordered. The insects sleep in prime numbers. They wake up to sing. They sing and they die and they do it again.

NOTES

All excerpts from Bashō's travel journal rely on Cid Corman's translation, *Back Roads to Far Towns: Bashō's Oku-No-Hosomichi* (1995).

Alison, Kian, and Argos are the real names of two real-ish people and a dog. This book's for them. It was written in New York, north Georgia, and at the University of Mississippi, where I received heaps of encouragement from the entire poetry faculty and many friends, especially Jan, Sarah, and Eric.

The italicized language in "5:36" is adapted from the decision in the case of Sid & Marty Krofft Television Productions Inc. v. McDonald's Corp. 562 F.2d 1157. 9th Cir. 1977, except "ketchup ketchup," which is something the birds say.

Individual lines of the italicized haiku in "7:31" are drawn from prose portions of *Back Roads to Far Towns*.

The song playing in the car in "7:59" is "Like Like the the the Death" by Silver Jews.

ANDREW DALLY writes poetry and code in Spartanburg, South Carolina. He holds an MFA from the University of Mississippi and, with the poet Jan Verberkmoes, runs a micro-press called Condensery.

※

COLOPHON

Text is set in a digital version of Jenson, designed by Robert Slimbach in 1996, and based on the work of punchcutter, printer, and publisher Nicolas Jenson. The titles here are in Futura.

❊

NEW MICHIGAN PRESS, based in Tucson, Arizona, prints poetry and prose chapbooks, especially work that transcends traditional genre. Together with DIAGRAM, NMP sponsors a yearly chapbook competition.

DIAGRAM, a journal of text, art, and schematic, is published bimonthly at THEDIAGRAM.COM. Periodic print anthologies are available from the New Michigan Press at NEWMICHIGANPRESS.COM.

CPSIA information can be obtained
at www.ICGtesting.com
Printed in the USA
BVHW072211290519
549538BV00001B/14/P

9 781934 832660